TWO HAIKU POETS

Annie Bachini

Helen Buckingham

First published 2023 by IRON Press
5 Marden Terrace, Cullercoats
North Shields, NE30 4PD
tel +44(0)191 2531901
ironpress@xlnmail.com
www.ironpress.co.uk

ISBN 9781-838344-4-1-2
Printed by Imprint Digital

© The poems, Annie Bachini and Helen Buckingham 2023
© This collection, IRON Press 2023

Cover and book design
Brian Grogan and Peter Mortimer

Typeset in Georgia 10pt

IRON Press books are distributed by
NBN International and represented by
Inpress Ltd, Milburn House, Dean Street
Newcastle upon Tyne NE1 1LF
tel: +44(0)191 2308104
www.inpressbooks.co.uk

ANNIE BACHINI has written haiku, tanka and renga since the 1990s. Many UK and international journals and anthologies have featured her haiku, including *The IRON Book of British Haiku*, IRON Press, 1998 and *Haiku in English: The First Hundred Years*, W. W. Norton & Company, Inc., 2013. For different periods of time she was newsletter editor, journal editor and president of the British Haiku Society. She runs workshops and has taught haiku in Adult Education. Her first collection, *the river's edge,* was published in 2003 by The Bare Bones Press.

HELEN BUCKINGHAM was born in London and currently lives in Wells, Somerset. She has been writing haiku and senryu for the past three decades. Collections include *water on the moon* (Original Plus, 2010) and *sanguinella* (Red Moon Press, 2017), each of which was shortlisted for a THF Touchstone Award. Anthologies include *The Humours of Haiku* (IRON Press, 2012) and *Haiku in English*: The First Hundred Years (W. W. Norton, 2013). In 2016 she won first prize in the Martin Lucas Haiku Award.

Page 8

74 Haiku
by Annie Bachini

Page 33

74 Haiku
by Helen Buckingham

Annie Bachini

——————— Two Haiku Poets ———————

an ordinary street
with people doing ordinary things
—the moon
                –After Hosomi Ayako

wind on my face
      fallen leaves
  shift a little

lurching to a halt
the weight of the bus
inside my body

Annie Bachini

a blackbird emerges
from under the car
and steps on fresh snow

Christmas Day
chirrups
from the construction site

locked down for three months
the old computer and I
not compatible

dappled path
quavers in my voice
not used for a while

an avenue of London planes
     how small
         I am

faint breeze rolling a scrunched paper bag

Annie Bachini

repairing the bridge
men in orange overalls
clump along planking

bare bulb
in a high-rise window
starless night

return to pre-covid
a shop doorway shelters
a homeless man

on a broken-down train buddleia alive and dead

waiting room
the rhythmic squeaks
of the cleaner's shoes

station platform
twins on short reins
peer down at the rails

Annie Bachini

so romantic
the song in French
fading bluebells

beneath the hedge
and shaded by it
mating snails

chasing a laugh
the clown student stumbles
on a creaking board

the wind going my way today

with each hat coin
the beatboxer
touches his heart

mountain snow
together perhaps
for the last time

Annie Bachini

briefly a yellow butterfly

day's end
the light
in puffs of cloud

spring cleaning
what mother did
each week

Two Haiku Poets

face to face
two wooden spoons
in the rack

my fingers
changing the shade inside
the bone china mug

not quite
one or the other
buds of summer

Annie Bachini

late sun lightening the flying gull's breast

second-hand clothes
a ladybird lands on
the camouflage jacket

seven years
to weave a basket
bees in the lilac

evacuated island in elders' voices

in mist
the ferry
on the far shore

toothache
briefly absorbed
by the full moon

Annie Bachini

a builder asks me why I'm smiling

locked into slots
at the village school
a line of colourful scooters

brush strokes the rhythm of rippling corn

mist lifting
birds on the bridge
become pigeons

once again today
freeing my winged sleeve
from a door handle

in the open space
where the lavender pot was
scurry of beetles

Annie Bachini

rustled leaves give the blackbird away

howling wind louder than the cat's miaow

bare tree
connecting
with my bones

a few flowers
    and buds remain
frozen in time

in the churchyard
after a while
we are silent

through swirling fog the nineteenth century

Annie Bachini

the moon
with its messy aura
less awesome tonight

another brave woman
unknown to me
until her obituary

we rest
near the drift of snow
still on the mountain

tight buds
people I used to know

at the end of the longest day white bindweed

awake
through the night
a solitary blackbird

Annie Bachini

summer downpour
the hanging broom stems
covered in snails

mid-air
bread for the swans
grabbed by starlings

rolling through water
    the child
        in a bubble

peace garden
   the wall
warm on my back

leaning as though listening Japanese anemone

cobblestones
outside the station
a whiff of diesel

Annie Bachini

first bite
into the samosa
lentils fall out

restless tied dog
opening and closing
the mini-market door

old street lamp lit by winter sun

grey city river
carrying its history
here and there

heavy rain
the man in front's
worn down heels

dental hospital
dead flies line
the light casings

Annie Bachini

cat in the garden untangling twilight

new neighbours
a thrush looks up at the feeder
no longer there

heatwave
little vapour puffs
from the wiped sills

the play of light
a ghostly sun
enters the room

like death carriage after carriage passes empty

internal flight
the cabin staff
older

Annie Bachini

low cloud the furrowed field full of gulls

grey dusk
masts barely visible
without their sails

again this visit
the same faces
at the village bus stop

festive season
amongst old gravestones
early daffodils

pause
in the fireworks
or is it the end

Helen Buckingham

Helen Buckingham

midnight sea sings a capella

world news
the moon
my rock

Earth Hour
ursa minor
steps up

child
lying
hand
to
mouth

    snowman
  down to his
last piece of coal

hunger moon
hovering over
the picket line

high table
a parliament of crows
breaking bread

stop press methane on Mars has legs

WHITEHALL
HOME OF ICE
     F

gallery shut
rain splashes
the sidewalk

Earthrise
not ours
to see

hugging ban
she cradles
his ashes

last kisses sealed behind glass

anniversary gift
lily-of-the-valley
perfuming his fist

midnight cries
    child mother
    child

cheating ministers hug it out

air ambulance
touches down; a whirlwind
of petals and grit

numbers
still climbing
cold mountain

── Helen Buckingham ──

May Day
the hill
short of breath

a cloud
breaks my fall
blossom snow

lockdown
lifted
by larksong

spring breeze
twirling my cardi
at the CCTV

wind drops —
the neighbour's cat
brings me petals

at the foot
of the fire escape
bluebells tremble

a trio
of mowers
silencing their lawns

sparkling spring water
... a washed-up label

street party
I hitch my dream
to a passing balloon

roof bathing
a mosaic of
beach towels

rainbow's end
no parking

en route to the doctor's
a stray bluebell...
my desire not to kick it

Helen Buckingham

hunched in a corner
of the waiting room
gibbous moon

newtabletsadnauseam

a cuckoo
in the sparrows' nest
solstice festival

holy island
no chorus
of sirens

sunlit nave
our shadows
dappled red

poached
in salt water...
midday sun

driftwood
she draws
a sad face

sea glass
the fragility

a scent
of star jasmine
night garden

dog days
the overheated air
their views

art school
fixing
the urinal

gallery café
the spider hangs
its work

Helen Buckingham

summer's end...
covid clinging
to its skirts

masked crocodile
crossing that bridge
back to school

teacher mouths dark matter

Two Haiku Poets

test clear –
she takes a deep breath
and rejoins the race

prodigal sun
the barbecue
back on

wannabe cowboy
one foot on the kissing gate
he lights up a vape

Helen Buckingham

lightning
our world
on a spit

bus stop roadkill follows me home

back to school
morning assembly
at the local Greasy Spoon

I'd like to teach the world...
we kick another coke can
down the road

last dance
all eyes on
each other

bin night
foxes recycle
skin and bone

Helen Buckingham

drive-thru
monoxide
sandwich

candlelit evening —
cold beans
straight from the tin

moving in gift bruised peaches

Halloween Night
something orange
parked in our place

joining me
at my lowest
perigee moon

Guy Fawkes'
the bonfire
splutters on

toddler chews
on a paper poppy
lest we forget

sparrow
carolling
me home

underground train
the city breathing
down my neck

   tree
    lights
  counting
those missing

stretch limo night
spangled
with stars

rifling through
my 5-yr diary
winter breeze

heads crack
together...
the beautiful game

open mic night:
the rain's
low patter

big thaw
mountain
to landfill

briefly
part of my own life
memorial swing

one last turn
around the moat
cold moon

out of grief
the morning sun
on my shoulder

Helen Buckingham

sickle moon
the old pub roof
losing its thatch

snowbound
the ghost train
ploughs on

Acknowledgements

Annie Bachini

Some of the haiku included in this collection were first published by the following journals and web pages: Blithe Spirit, Blōō Outlier, Ginyu-haiku, Haiku Corner, Lacewings, Presence and tsuri-dōrō. Thanks to the editors of these journals, the following anthology editors and others who have chosen my poems: Haïku *sans frontières*: une anthologie mondiale, Les Éditions David, 1998; *Haiku Troubadours 2000*, Ginyu Press; *The New Haiku*, Snapshot Press, 2002; *big sky*: The Red Moon Anthology of English Language Haiku, 2006; *echoes 1*, Red Moon Press, 2007; *Kamesan's World Haiku Anthology on War, Violence and Human Rights Violation*, 2013; International 'Kusamakura' Haiku Competition (2nd prize) 2014; echoes 2, Red Moon Press, 2018; *Wishbone Moon*, Jacar Press, 2018. Thanks also to Dee Evetts, Steve Mason, Matthew Paul and Dick Pettit for helping me choose my initial submission to IRON Press.

Helen Buckingham

With thanks to the editors of the following publications in which these poems first appeared. *Acorn, Blithe Spirit, Bones, The British Haiku Society Members' Anthology: Temple, Chrysanthemum, Consulate-General of Japan in Toronto: Sakura Haiku Challenge, DailyHaiku, FemkuMag, Frogpond, The Haiku Foundation, The Heron's Nest, A Hundred Gourds, is/let, The Journal, The Mainichi, Modern Haiku, Moongarlic, NOON: journal of the short poem, Otata, Presence, Prune Juice, Pulse, tinywords, tsuri-doro, Wales Haiku Journal.*

AWARD
'world news' (The Tenth Annual Peggy Willis Lyles Haiku Awards, Hon. Mention, 2022)